DISGRACE

FEMINISM

&

THE POLITICAL RIGHT

A SERIES OF 12 ETCHINGS BY

HANNAH QUINLAN &

ROSIE HASTINGS

FEATURING 3 ESSAYS BY

AKANKSHA MEHTA

LOLA OLUFEMI

JULIET JACQUES

ARCADIA MISSA PUBLICATIONS

Arcadia Missa Publications
35 Duke Street
London
W1U 1LH

www.arcadiamissa.com
@ArcadiaMissa
info@arcadiamissa.com

Disgrace: Feminism & the Political Right

ISBN: 978-1-8382840-3-9

Arcadia Missa Publications are available from the
gallery, our website and selected stockists

Disgrace: Feminism & the Political Right

RUTH PILSTON

Disgrace: Feminism and the Political Right explores the history of conservative feminism in the UK from the Edwardian period to today. Conceived as an accompaniment to Hannah Quinlan and Rosie Hastings' eponymous exhibition, the book aims to provide contextual information for the viewer, both as a resource on the history of feminism on the political right and to provide a deeper historical and political insight into the works within the exhibition.

On view at Arcadia Missa in September 2021, *Disgrace* presents a recent body of work by the artists including a fresco painting; a film work; two coloured pencil drawings and a series of twelve etchings. At the centre of the exhibition, the etchings are an attempt by the artists to construct a specific feminist timeline, mapping the connections between the various historical manifestations of conservative feminism that lead to the current moment.

The book itself centres around this timeline, with three essays covering what the artists have identified as three significant time periods for conservative feminism. Accompanying etchings that allegorise women's movements in the period leading up to WWII, an essay by Akanksha Mehta, a lecturer in Gender, Sexuality, and Cultural Studies and the co-director of the Centre for Feminist Research at Goldsmiths, considers the nature of the women's suffrage movement, focusing on the relationship between the suffragettes and eugenics discourse. A polemical text by Lola Olufemi, a black feminist writer and organiser with the London Feminist Library, questions the women's liberation movement and 'sex wars' of the mid 20th century. In the final essay – alongside etchings exploring 'free-market feminism', Theresa May's 'Women2Win' campaign and the proliferation of transphobic rhetoric – writer, filmmaker and journalist Juliet Jacques uses Caryl Churchill's innovative 1982 play 'Top Girls' to trace the trajectory of women in power, from Thatcher into the future of feminism.

*

It was the scenes played out in Jacques text – the trans-exclusionary and free-market feminisms outlined in the final etchings – that the artists took as a starting point for their show and for the research it embodies. Whilst many contemporary feminisms are intersectional, liberationist and abolitionist, white feminism, and the colonial classism from which it is constructed, is embedded in the politics of today with many movements, including those positioned within supposedly left-wing political parties, closely aligned with conservative, right-wing and fascist politics.

In 2019, the second female Prime Minister of the United Kingdom of Great Britain and Northern Ireland, Theresa May, stepped down. As Prime Minister, she had struggled through Brexit negotiations and lost the Conservative Party's majority at a general election, clinging onto power through a deal brokered with the right-wing homophobic, anti-abortion Democratic Unionist Party. In her previous position as Home Secretary, May was responsible for the formation of the 'hostile environment' and called for the UK's withdrawal from the European convention on human rights, as a means to further persecute 'illegal immigrants'.[1] Before joining the Conservative front-bench, May co-founded the campaign group *Women2Win* – depicted in Quinlan and Hastings' etching *I'm not a woman I'm a conservative* – which 'aims to increase the number of

1. Travis, A. *What does Theresa May's record as home secretary tell us?* 2016. The Guardian.

4

Conservative women in Parliament and in public life'[2] and was photographed in 2006 wearing a 'This is what a feminist looks like' tshirt, promoted by the Fawcett Society, the UK's leading charity campaigning for gender equality.[3]

May's departure as PM made space for Boris Johnson, a self-described feminist whose history of misogyny, homophobia and racism is well-documented.[4] During his premiership, Johnson's policies have reflected these ideologies: his government has failed to move forward with reforms of the Gender Recognition Act and banning conversion therapy; his coronavirus response has entrenched existing inequalities, placing the brunt of the economic fallout on women's shoulders,[5] and has killed a disproportionate number of BAME people and disabled people[6]; and his government has brought in further restrictions on immigration, led by an advocate of the Women2Win campaign,[7] the Home Secretary Priti Patel.

Patel and Johnson's government more generally seems to intend to take the asylum system into an increasingly draconian direction, with a new 'Nationality and Borders Bill' that aims to roll back the UK's commitments to the 1951 Refugee Convention, putting the lives of people seeking safety in the UK at risk.[8] The inflammatory rhetoric of 'invasion',[9] used to describe refugees making the dangerous journey across the channel, feeds into expressions of British identity, embedded in imperial sentiment, historical circumstances and we-shall-fight-them-on-the-beaches war nostalgia.[10] This aggressive political rhetoric, this 'othering', results in the villainization of minority groups, in this instance migrants, in order to divert the dominant group's attention from more complex

2. Women2Win. *About Us.* (https://www.women2win.com/about-us)

3. Fawcett Society (https://www.flickr.com/photos/fawcettsociety/3115868250)

4. *Beastliness, beatings, buses & blunders.* 2019. The Guardian.

5. Preskey, N. Gallagher, S. & Hall H. *The pandemic of inequality: How coronavirus is setting women's rights back decades.* 2021. The Independent.

6. Siddique, H. *UK ministers accused over impact of Covid on minorities and disabled people.* 2020. The Guardian.

7. Women2WinCampaign. *Priti Patel, MP for Witham, talks to Women2Win about the realities of being an MP.* 2011. (https://www.youtube.com/watch?v=2vB_66oN1qI)

8. Rahman, M. *The gal-dem guide to Priti Patel's horrible new immigration bill.* 2021. gal-dem Magazine.

9. Stewart, C. *Priti Patel's migrant 'invasion' is war language from a government losing on all fronts.* 2020. The Herald.

10. Baker, T. A. *The othering of migrants has negative consequences for society at large.* 2020. LSE Blog.

economic and social issues.[11]

It is this process of othering, this notion of 'us' and 'them', that Quinlan and Hastings see mirrored in the conflicts within certain contemporary feminisms; the language of the refugee 'invasion' reflected in the so-called 'gender-critical' rhetoric of a 'trans epidemic,'[12] allegorised in the etching *We Will Not Be Silenced*. In an essay published by the White Pube, artist and writer Linda Stupart outlines the way in which transphobia and right-wing racism are linked through a mutual process of othering, whether that is the British public supporting off-shore detention centres over an exaggerated perception of the economic and cultural threat of immigration; or Nina Power (the former women and migrants' rights activist Stupart's text centres on), charities like Woman's Place UK, or journalists like Julie Burchill and Suzanne Moore[13] scapegoating trans women through their own white-victimhood. As Stupart writes in the text, 'this victim status becomes so central to an understanding of self, that this trauma-identity becomes individualised, paranoid, and exclusionary, and thus weaponised against other (often more) marginalised people ... The white woman's victim status (that same victim status that was also responsible for the historic murder and continued vilification of black men) is preserved only at the cost of an Other's."[14]

However, as Quinlan and Hastings hope to outline in their exhibition, this is not new to feminism. The trajectory of western feminism has long been propelled by a right-wing element, lifted up on the oppression of others. In the etching, *Tea, garden & evening parties, rifle competitions, polo matches, the trooping of the colours and other special events*, we see a group playing a party game on a lawn, a nod to the events and excursions held by

11. Looney, S. *Breaking Point? An Examination of the Politics of Othering in Brexit Britain.* 2017. TLI Think!

12. Pavia, W. *Author Abigail Shrier faces threats after warning of trans epidemic.* 2020. The Times.

13. Kaveney, R. *Julie Burchill has ended up bullying the trans community.* 2013. The Guardian.

14. Stupart, L. *On Trauma.* The White Pube.

conservative colonial organisations like the Primrose League and the Victoria League for Commonwealth Friendship. In *Imperial Ladies Auxiliary,* we see a middle-class woman holding a globe in one hand, a working woman dressing her in a cloak. These etchings depict women's complicity in the British imperial project, a project in which women – like suffragettes Milicent Fawcett and Emmeline Pankhurst; members of the Victoria and Primrose Leagues; or the explorer Isabella Bird, fictionalised in *Top Girls* – played a significant role.

*

In a paper exploring the role Fawcett, and the feminist vision she stood for, played in the Boer War, academic and Kingston University professor Vron Ware wrote, 'In many ways, Victorian feminism was a product of the British Empire and the philanthropic impulse of many female activists... was to support the spread of white, Christian civilisation to the furthest reaches of the earth, especially if it meant liberating native women from customs and habits regarded as barbarous and uncivilised" [15] Ware goes on to describe the implications of this, in today's feminist histories·

' *large sections of the suffrage movement absorbed and embraced militaristic notions of duty and service to the nation in return for the promise of citizenship, abandoning feminism's radical potential as a peace-making project that sought justice through arbitration as well as liberty for all, without distinction of race, colour or sex. Mainstream accounts of Fawcett's achievements today effectively brush aside the logic of this feminist pact with the norms and social practices that sustain militarism.'* [16]

15. Ware, V. *All the rage: decolonizing the history of the British women's suffrage movement.* 2020. Cultural Studies, 34:4, 521-545

16. Ibid.

Fawcett and the more militant Women's Social and Political Union continued their support of military action during the First World War, when their suffrage campaign paused so members could support the war effort. While middle-class suffragettes began entering many different areas of work that had previously been the domain of men and working-class women, one notable expansion of women's work into the realm of militarism was the Women's Police Service, founded in August 1914 by Nina Boyle and Margaret Damer Dawson. Damer Dawson had an enthusiasm for police enforcement that was shared with Mary Sophia Allen, a suffragette and voluntary police officer with whom she 'established a close professional and personal relationship, living together in London between 1914 and 1920.'[17] Paying special attention to law affecting women and children, the Women's Police Service (depicted in the etching *Women's Police Volunteers*) were particularly concerned over 'the increase in prostitution'[18] and 'protecting young women from the temptations of urban life',[19] until 1919 when women began to formally enter police forces.

Coinciding with the end of the First World War, in 1918, the Representation of the People Act was passed in the UK which enfranchised women over the age of 30, who owned property themselves, or were married to a property owner. Fawcett believed the war played a key part in the suffrage movement, writing:

'The war temporarily suspended the progress of the suffrage movement, but it is probable that it ultimately strengthened the demand of women for citizenship, for it has been observed again and again that a war, or any other event that stimulates national vitality, and the consciousness of the value of citizenship is almost certain to be followed by increased vigour in the suffrage movement, and not infrequently by its success.'[20]

17. Simkin, J. *Mary Allen*. 1997/2020. Spartacus Educational.

18. Woodeson, A. *The first women police: a force for equality or infringement?* 1993. Women's History Review, 2:2, 217-232.

19. Staveley-Wadham, R. *Policing Pioneers – A Look at the History of the Women's Police Service.* 2021. The British Newspaper Archive.

20. Fawcett, M.G. *Women's Suffrage: A Short History of a Great Movement.* 1912. CreateSpace Independent Publishing Platform, 69-70.

But, although the Representation of the People Act left many people still disenfranchised, for middle-class women like Fawcett – whose statue was erected in Parliament Square to celebrate the centenary of the Act – this meant an end to their need to struggle for suffrage. Fawcett left the movement in 1919; Rosa May Billinghurst, the disabled suffragette discussed in Akanksha Mehta's text, stopped campaigning after the Act came into law; and Emmeline Pankhurst (whose campaign for enfranchisement for female property owners earned the nickname 'Votes for Ladies',[21] referenced in Quinlan and Hastings' eponymous etching) disbanded the Women's Social and Political Union in 1918. Many former suffragettes stood in the 1918 General Election, including Christabel Pankhurst, Emmeline Pethick-Lawrence and Norah Elam, but only Irish revolutionary, socialist and suffragist Constance Markievicz was elected.

21. Jackson, S. *'Women quite unknown': working-class women in the suffrage movement.* 2018. The British Library.

As an imprisoned member of the Irish republican party Sinn Fein, Markievicz refused to take her seat in the UK's parliament; instead, the first woman to do so was Lady Nancy Astor, an anti-semitic and anti-catholic Conservative politician, who vocally supported Hitler and Nazi Germany. Commandant of the Women's Police Service, Margaret Damer Dawson commended her election, writing in the Hull Daily Mail, 'I heartily congratulate Lady Astor on her election to the House of Commons. The large majority that she has gained shows that the time is now ripe for women generally to take their place in the government of the country.'[22]

22. Staveley-Wadham, R. *Policing Pioneers – A Look at the History of the Women's Police Service.* 2021. The British Newspaper Archive.

Though Astor herself had not campaigned for votes for women, there were many former suffragettes who found themselves drawn to similar politics and similar movements. Once held in Holloway prison with the founder of the Women's Social and Political Union, Emmeline Pankhurst, for their militant direct action for suffrage, Norah Elam was one such suffragette who turned to fascism, campaigning for the internment of 'enemy aliens' after WWI and then joining the British Union of Fascists in the early 1930s. In 1940, Elam returned to Holloway with Diana Mosley, Mitford sister and wife of BUF leader Oswald Mosley, this time for her National Socialist sympathies.[23]

For many activists like Elam, the British Union of Fascists seemed a natural successor to the Women's Social and Political Union. 'I was first attracted to the Blackshirts because I saw in them the courage, the action, the loyalty, the gift of service, and the ability to serve which I had known in the suffragette movement,'[24] explained Mary Richardson, a former militant suffragette (noted for vandalising the *Rokeby Venus*[25]) who alongside Elam and former voluntary police officer Mary Sophia Allen, became the 'Lady Blackshirts' of Quinlan and Hastings' etching, involved in the rising nationalist, anti-semitic fascist movement in the UK.

*

But it was not only the idea of war-like service that attracted these feminists to National Socialism and the BUF. 'Eugenic theory was a basic and formative, not an incidental, part of feminist positions on the vitally important themes of motherhood, reproduction, and the state,'[26] historian Ann Taylor Allen writes in a comparative paper on Feminism and Eugenics in Germany and Britain between 1900 and 1940. Taylor Allen continues, 'the ethical problem that underlay feminist support for the eugenics was... their failure to embed arguments for women's rights in a comprehensive understanding

23. Durham, M. *Women and Fascism.* 1998. Routledge, 43–51.

24. Ricardson, M. *The Blackshirt.* 1934.

25. BBC News. *Rokeby Venus: The painting that shocked a suffragette.* 2014.

26. Taylor Allen, A. *Feminism and Eugenics in Germany and Britain, 1900-1940: A Comparative Perspective.* 2000. German Studies Review, Vol. 23, No. 3, 477-505.

of human rights.' In an explicit example, Christabel Pankhurst used eugenic arguments to support her feminist militancy; she wrote in *The Suffragette* in 1914, if men do not reform, 'the worst fears of the eugenicists will be fulfilled and the race bred entirely from inferior stock'.[27] In 1923, Emmeline Pankhurst, Christabel's mother and former dictatorial leader of WSPU, toured North America, speaking about national and racial health, emphasising the importance of marriage between healthy individuals, as part of an educational campaign by the National Council for Combating Venereal Disease[28] (an institution whose eugenicist founder Sybil Neville-Rolfe is discussed in Mehta's text).

'The absence of the human-rights perspective,' Taylor Allen notes, 'on reproductive rights led feminists to support some measures that victimized not only men but women as well.'[29] While we also see the absence of a human-rights perspective in Fawcett's promotion of concentration camps in the Boer War,[30] it is often, as Taylor Allen writes, in reproductive freedoms that these feminisms fall short. Early campaigns for access to contraception and safe abortion, although now positioned as an important part of women's liberation, were cached in the language of eugenics, in population control, as represented in the etching *Social Hygeine.*[31]

*

Just as the Women's Police Service or the Primrose League were borne from a compulsion to propagate a specific idea of womanhood, what Vron Ware describes as 'the philanthropic impulse ... to support the spread of white, Christian civilisation',[32] we see comparable impulses play out in later feminisms.

27. Pankhurst, C. *Concerning Damaged Goods.* 1914. The Suffragette, in Taylor Allen, A. *Feminism and Eugenics in Germany and Britain, 1900-1940: A Comparative Perspective.* 2000. German Studies Review, Vol. 23, No. 3, 477-505.

28. Kubergovic, E. *Pankhurst, Emmeline.* 2013. Eugenics Archive Canada.

29. Taylor Allen, A. ibid. 2000. German Studies Review, Vol. 23, No. 3, 477-505.

30. Ware, V. ibid. 2020. Cultural Studies, 04.4, 521-545

31. Taylor Allen, A. ibid. 2000. German Studies Review, Vol. 23, No. 3, 477-505.

32. Ware, V. ibid. 2020. Cultural Studies, 34:4, 521-545

In the late 1970s and the 1980s, we see the return of campaigns against sex-work, which had been promoted in the first half of the century by groups like the National Council for Combating Venereal Disease, the Eugenics Society and the Women's Police Service (who promoted a curfew for all women as a means to curb sex-work and other 'disorderly' behaviour).[33] In 1976, the group known as *Women Against Violence in Pornography and Media* was formed in the USA, with figures such as Andrea Dworkin, Catherine MacKinnon and Adrienne Rich calling for an end to pornography, pushing aside questions of sex-workers' bodily autonomy and labour rights.[34] Writing about the clash between sex-positive campaigners and anti-pornography feminists in the 1980s, Lola Olufemi asks 'How much of the sex wars was protecting femininity as imbued in the body of white women, a desire to protect virtue, virginity's successor.' How much of what drives the likes of Andrea Dworkin and other 'anti-porn' protestors is Ware's 'philanthropic impulse', borne out of the logic of generations of white colonial feminist thought?

In their 1984 essay, 'Challenging Imperial Feminism', for the *Feminist Review*, Valerie Amos and Pratibha Parmar discuss the problem with this: 'very often women's oppression is seen in a straightforward and non-contradictory way, where women organizing as women is seen as positive, regardless of the context. An example of such reasoning taken to its extreme is when some white feminists have applauded Maggie Thatcher as Prime Minister as a positive female image,'[35] or when, as in the etching *Sex Wars,* some white feminists 'protect women', regardless of whether or not they want protecting.

33. Woodeson, A. *The first women police: a force for equality or infringement?* 1993. Women's History Review, 2:2, 217-232.

34. McBride, J. *The Sex Wars, 1970s to 1980s. 2008.* Out History.

35. Amos, V. and Parmar, P. *Challenging Imperial Feminism.* 1984. Feminist Review, no. 17, 3–19.

As depicted in the etching *Free-market,* this is a kind of feminism that persists, a kind of corporate feminism that places the desires of certain women above others, that prioritises "'making women Prime Minister" over improving the lives of working people,'[36] that celebrates women in high places but ignores the pile of bodies beneath them. Journalist Dawn Foster wrote of this in her 2015 criticism of 'trickle-down feminism', *Lean Out:*

36. Jacques, J.

'The problem with corporate feminism's obsession with individual stories of success, and "having it all", is that many women don't have much at all. Women have been disproportionately affected by austerity... A few more women may be MPs or CEOs, but three times as many young women are locked into low-paid jobs than were 20 years ago.'[37]

37. Foster, D. *Lean Out.* 2016. Repeater Books.

As Juliet Jacques states in her essay, 'May's main legacy has been to cement the idea that the Tories can use minorities to cover for policies that are disastrous for those minorities.'[38] With Theresa May's feminism little more than witty come-backs at the dispatch box – and earlier female politicians like Lady Astor and Thatcher upholding no feminist agenda – the suggestion that the way to liberation is more women in power has long been proven false.

38. Jacques, J.

*

Here, and in Quinlan and Hastings' exhibition, we have outlined a history of feminism as it intersects and entwines with the violence and oppression of colonialism, capitalism and neoliberalism. Like the characters in the opening scene of Caryl Churchill's *Top Girls,* the figures in these etchings, and these narratives more generally, have long been those lauded for their contribution to women's rights – Millicent Fawcett memorialised with a statue in Parliament Square, Lady Astor towering over Plymouth Hoe, a 10ft bronze Margaret Thatcher to be installed in Grantham later this year ('they blow those fascists up so big'[39]) – but these aren't the only feminists. In her essay, Akanksha Mehta describes exasperation at a tendency within white feminist discourse, performance lectures, exhibitions such as this one, to linger on these histories.

39. Olufemi, L.

'Feminist history charges us, as women committed to the liberation of women, to know the past in order to consider what we want to conserve and what we want not to repeat or continue,'[40] said Adrienne Rich (her own feminist credentials brought into question today for gender essentialism[41]) in a 1983 lecture 'Resisting Amnesia: History and Personal Life'. She continued:

40. Rich, A. *Blood, bread and poetry.* 1987. Virago Press, 146.

41. Mukhopadhya, S. *Was Adrienne Rich Anti-Trans?* 2012. The American Prospect.

'Women have been writing women's history - and feminist history - for several centuries; it is not a new invention, but is has been ignored, buried, erased over and over. Each new generation of feminists has been forced to document the most elementary exposition of the oppression of women yet again and also to repeat mistakes made by sisters of an earlier era.'[42]

42. Rich, A. ibid. 1987. Virago Press, 147.

In 'Challenging Imperial Feminism', Valerie Amos and Pratibha Parmar expanded on this sentiment, away from a white women's history, writing:

'The 'herstory' which white women use to trace the roots of women's oppression or to justify some form of political practice is an imperial history rooted in the prejudices of colonial and neo-colonial periods, a 'herstory' which suffers the same form of historical amnesia of white male

14

historians, by ignoring the fundamental ways in which white women have benefitted from the oppression of Black people.' [43]

43. Amos, V. and Parmar, P. ibid. 1984. Feminist Review, no. 17, 3–19.

Amos and Parmar continue:

'True feminist theory and practice entails an understanding of imperialism and a critical engagement with challenging racism - elements which the current women's movement significantly lacks, but which are intrinsic to Black feminism.' [44]

44. Ibid.

In her essay, Akanksha Mehta outlines a telling of 'herstory' – 'the kind of white gendered history that allows white women to stand proudly with placards that say ridiculous things like 'well behaved women rarely make history''[45] – that omits different feminist narratives, narratives 'about women who fought for freedom from Empire and from racism, about women in trade union movements and working class women fighting for the vote and much more, about Black women fighting white supremacy and patriarchy and imagining and realising queer kinships and worlds, about transnational sisterhoods between Black, brown, Muslim, colonised, migrant, working-class, disabled women'.[46] The list of what Lola Olufemi thinks of as 'women's lib' is not Fawcett and Thatcher but 'THOSE LESBIANS THAT ABSEILED INTO THE HOUSES OF PARLIAMENT AND AUDRE LORDE'S READING GROUP IN BERLIN'.[47]

45. Mehta, A.

46. Ibid.

47. Olufemi, L.

This series of etchings by Quinlan and Hastings 'serves as a warning', as Juliet Jacques writes of Caryl Churchill's play, 'not to repeat this privileging of "making women Prime Minister" over improving the lives of working people, and not to allow the Conservatives to repeat the same trick with feminism, or with racial or sexual minorities.'[48] *Disgrace* 'charges us, as women committed to the liberation of women, to know the past in order to consider what we want to conserve and what we want not to repeat or continue.'[49]

'Listen closely, can you hear the echoes?'

48. Jacques, J.

49. Rich, A. ibid. 1987. Virago Press, 146.

50. Olufemi, L.

Tea, Garden & Evening Parties, Rifle Competitions,
Polo Matches, The Trooping of the Colours and
Other Special Events

Pre-Existing Conditions: Feminisms, Empire, Futures

Akanksha Mehta

Part I – Remember/Honour/Shock

I have crossed under the railway bridge on Elmira Street in Ladywell, Lewisham, a dozen times in the last year but, on a late night in mid-July, on my way back home from a friend's house, I noticed the mural in pinks, purples, greens, and white for the first time. A car drove by, splashing water on my shoes. In the light I saw, *NOW IS THE TIME*. I crossed the road. *VOTES FOR WOMEN*. Some women drawn in full – one woman using a wheelchair featured prominently – and others as sprawling swirls. I looked it up right then. The mural was called 'A Thousand Feet Will Follow' and honours Rosa May Billinghurst, a disabled suffragette born in Lewisham.[1] Artmongers, who painted the mural in only two weeks, write that she was 'famous for her mischievous use of her wheelchair during protests. Yes, there was window smashing.'[2] The Women's Social and Political Union gave her a 'Hunger Strike Medal for valour'; she spent months in Holloway Prison; she also supported prioritising the [imperial] war over the campaign for the vote [for white middle class women].[3] I walked towards New Cross, trying to pay attention to the song on my headphones.

Years ago, I clicked one too many times and regretfully ended up on a page on the Museum of London's website called *'The Suffragettes'. Militant. Art. Propaganda. Protest. Destruction. Strike. 'Edwardian' London. Gatherings. Arrests. Wake Up the Nation. Actions. Demonstrations. First World War. Suspension of Militancy. Vote. Propertied.*[4] [Yikes! You're missing a few words huh? How about Race? Empire? Imperialism?] There was a photograph of a pendant. Silver with purple, green, and white stones. It was presented to a suffragette, arrested in Parliament Square, upon her release from Holloway Prison. She

1. *Finishing touches made to long awaited mural celebrating Lewisham's suffragettes.* 2019. Ladywell Live.

2. For images and more about the mural on the Artmongers website (www.artmongersaction.org/all-projects/a-thousand-feet-will-follow)

3. Read more about Rosa May Billinghurst in this NYT profile: Fielding, S. *Overlooked No More: Rosa May Billinghurst, Militant Suffragette.* 2020. The New York Times.

4. *The Suffragettes.* Museum of London. (https://www.museumoflondon.org.uk/discover/suffragettes)

was given a 'royal welcome', greeted at the prison gates by other members of Kensington Women's Social and Political Union and gifted the pendant, a tiny depiction of a winged figure of 'Hope' singing outside the prison bars. They said her husband encouraged her to become a suffragette. He was a GP. The pendant is on display. *Production Date: 1909.* [5] The details stuck.

Remember the time when a fancy university in London renamed three campus buildings to honour famous British suffragettes? [I wonder if these were near the building/cafe named after a prominent male eugenicist? They'd all get on quite well of course.] The article announcing this *unveiling* had a photograph with many, actually all, white women smiling outside the newly-titled building. Dressed like the suffragettes [I assume], one of them held a sign in purple, white, green – *well behaved women rarely make history.* [6] [Oh dear! Not that trite white woman nonsense again. Down the road from this institution, in the shops for tourists, they sell fridge magnets with that line nowadays.]

A few months into a new job, I was forced to attend and part-organise a talk – apologies, as the white feminist queer artist called it, *a performance lecture* – about a suffragette who smashed a portrait of racist and anti-abolitionist writer Thomas Carlyle in the National Portrait Gallery. Six days in Holloway Prison and she even tried to bravely get back into the gallery; that the portrait she destroyed was of a racist and antisemitic man who re-advocated for slavery after abolition was a mere co-incidence, she claimed; her *ill* behaviour had nothing to do with *those* histories; to the suffragette, he was just a man, who like so many, wrote women out of *our* history and founded the gallery and she was angry. [7] *But was this supposedly random act one of feminist fate?*

5. For images and more about the pendant in the Museum of London Collection (https://collections. museumoflondon.org.uk/ online/object/300365.html)

6. *LSE renames Towers after suffrage campaigners.* 2018. LSE NEWS. Also see this on Eugenics and the LSE – Dilawri, S. *Eugenics and the Academy in Britain: Confronting Historical Amnesia at the LSE.* 2019. Decolonising LSE Collective.

7. You can read more about this in the following article – Brown, M. *'Hatchet fiend' suffragette celebrated by National Portrait Gallery in London.* 2018. The Guardian.

The artist asked passionately in the 'explosive' two hours they had with us. *Did you know that the National Portrait Gallery is filled with portraits of racists and colonisers? Did you know that the gallery was founded by three racist colonisers and their busts still feature above the entrance? Did you know? Isn't it shocking? Want to know what is even more shocking? One of the founders of the gallery was responsible for the criminalisation of homosexuality in other parts of the world, like in India? Wow, did you know, they inherited those homophobic laws from the coloniser? Did you also know many of the suffragettes were themselves racist and part of the eugenicist and imperial and colonial project? Did you know that history is filled with feminists who were actually white supremacist?* A whole event – sorry again, performance lecture – drawn on the affect of white shock, innocence, and ignorance [8] and the pathetic pride of it all packaged as the presenting of 'accessible, emotional, entertaining, inclusive histories [f*** off] that have been hidden' [for whom? by whom?] and the 'queering' [stop, please] of 'chronicles' [ugh]. On my walk, I could almost feel my headache from the night of the event [of course, I mean performance lecture] return. I reached home just as it stopped raining.

8. For more on 'white shock' and 'white innocence' see – Salem, S. *White Innocence as a Feminist Discourse: Intersectionality, and the 2016 US Presidential Elections.* 2018. in *Antagonizing White Feminism; Intersectionality's Critique of Women's Studies and the Academy,* editors Noelle Chaddock and Beth Hinderliter. Lexington books; and Wekker, G. *White innocence: paradoxes of colonialism and race.* 2016. Duke University Press.

The [white] artists emailed me and explained that they were doing an exhibition that explored the history of conservative white feminism from the Edwardian period to the current political moment. We are interested, they said, in the ways in which contemporary white feminist narratives situate historical feminisms within the politically radical left, omitting a long history of feminist affiliations with the political right, conservative politics, white supremacy and the empire. That sounds like a good exhibition and a worthy political project, I thought, but who is this actually for? Hasn't enough been said and done on this? Are we still having to tell the story of how *all* white feminism is/was a project of imperialism that not only invests itself in and emerges from racialised hierarchies and colonial violence but also, by virtue of that, only ever confines and kills the possibilities of gender justice and liberation?

I went on to look up 'Edwardian England' [I had no clue what that even was] and here is what I found out with every click: *The status of 'women' rose during this time and feminist struggles were at the forefront. 'Women' were active in the church and did a lot of social work, missionary work, teaching, pastoral and care work but had no role in leadership and this made them angry. They began to fight for their space in church affairs. Of course, this meant that they also actively avoided speaking about contraception and abortion – which were issues that 'women' saw to do only with promiscuous and poorer women. Working-class women were encouraged by 'women' to have illegal and unsafe abortions to prevent poverty and unemployment and contraceptives were tested on them. The size of [some] families decreased. 'Women' had more employment opportunities as there were now telephones, sewing machines, and*

typewriters in the world. Nursing emerged. School systems
expanded. 'Women' began to wear two-piece bathing suits
and high-waisted skirts and deeper necklines and play
sports professionally. More education, more magazines,
more femininity, more information, more Empire. Single
mothers got poorer and working-class women had limited
or no access to healthcare and terrible conditions of work.
'Women' fought for 'women's' suffrage. Women's Social
and Political Union started and its campaigns were public,
militant, disruptive, and demonstrative. 'Women' wanted a
political voice for 'women'. [9]

9. To read more, just google 'women in Edwardian England'

While white feminists today will speak of these 'radical
histories', what is often omitted is that this fight for a
'political voice for women' had everything to do with
Empire. British colonial violence and theft was always
gendered (military conquests coded as masculine and
metaphors of domesticity, home, family, femininity
coding the mission of 'civilising' and settlement) [10]
and relied on white middle-class and elite women's
crucial role as 'mothers' and 'daughters' of Empire. At
the beginning of the twentieth century, in this time of
supposed political and social change, women began
to contribute in more organised ways to the project
of Empire. Imperialist organisations (some that were
calling themselves feminist, others using words like
'women' or 'female' or 'girls' or 'ladies', many with
members who were also fighting for the vote and for
liberation of 'women') were set up and became crucial
to everyday political work. These organisations, such
as Girls' Friendly Society, the Primrose League (which
included the membership of several working-class
women), the British Women's Emigration Association,
and the Victoria League, were led by elite and middle-
class women but also drew in other 'respectable' women.
Their work was crucial for the spread and solidification

10. For more see: McClintock, A. *Imperial Leather. Race, Gender and Sexuality in the Colonial Contest.* 1995. Routledge.

of imperialist propaganda and narratives, for colonial education (at home and abroad), for lobbying and support, for expansion of the church, for guiding settlement in the colonies, for building relationships with colonial officials and acceptable 'natives'. [11]

Women, as leaders of these organisations, worked in a very organised, hierarchical, centralised, and networked manner to support the imperial project and had close relationships with the men who were the governing elite. Their personal engagements arose from a variety of motivations, not the least their need to assert their class-gender-racial positions and expand their already existing power, influence, and belief in the Christian colonial agenda. Their social worlds included travelling to the colonies, learning and becoming knowledgeable about what was going on 'over there', becoming 'experts' on feminised aspects of Empire, creating spaces of socialisation and leisure where they could come together, and drawing on, strengthening, and wanting a stake in the male dominions of imperial power. [12]

In England, these organisations were centred in London and heavily focussed on the 'civilising mission'. Politically active women promoted Christian morals (remember, they wanted to be leaders in church affairs too); supported missionary work by women (building of churches, emigration and settlement of women in the colonies, fund-raising etc.); demanded women's representation in political systems and the work-place and were invested in organised forms of philanthropy (as Christian moral duty) by and for women. Packaged as an escape from Victorian moral repression, English patriarchal oppression, and class-based society, settlement and emigration was promoted to both middle-class and working class women (the latter as

11. For a comprehensive history of Edwardian women's imperialist organisations, see Bush, J. *Edwardian Ladies and Imperial Power* (Women, Power, Politics). 2000. Leicester University Press.

12. For more, see the abovementioned work by Bush, J and Riedi, E. L. *Imperialist women in Edwardian Britain: the Victoria League, 1899-1914.* 2000. PhD Thesis, St Andrews University

there was demand for labour in the settlements). Entire programmes of education were drafted and delivered by women who knew that the colonial project was one of knowledge production and wanted to contest male-dominated narratives. Through this work of colonial education, charity, settlement, socialisation, and organising, women wanted to feminise the face of Empire and open up spaces of socio-cultural and political change and renewal. In attempts to contest existing gender relations within England (while and through wanting to maintain imperial and domestic gender-race-class hierarchies), women during the Edwardian era used these organisations to participate actively and indirectly in colonial violence while also claiming to fight for 'their' rights as 'women'.[13]

13. Again, see Bush, J (2000) and Riedi, E. L. (1998)

Managing differences between these organisations and between women involved in them was a key aspect of this time. At several points, tensions in political opinions were resolved by recognising that the colonial project was to supersede all others (and this is how these organisations contained anti-suffrage and pro-suffrage campaigners). Internationally, politically active women, fought for the creation of a 'sisterhood'; they went on tours and travels and hosted visitors, they offered support and knowledge to their 'sisters' that had settled and emigrated in the colonies and their organisation; they worked to form transnational networks of white womanhood. Empire was a project of racist global domination and they wanted to ensure their 'sisterhood' played a key role in this. It is unsurprising that their ideas of 'sisterhood' were based on race, eugenics, and white supremacy. Empire was cultural work; Empire was political work; Empire was biological work. What women were to populate the white settler colonies and what women were allowed to reproduce there? What women were to have smaller families to 'alleviate' poverty and unemployment? What women were to become mothers? What was to remain part of the civilising mission and the internationalist life of this political work by women and what was deemed unimportant? Are white feminists and white sisterhood ever really anything other than a project of imperial supremacy and racial domination, both 'at home' and 'abroad'? [14]

I think here of Sybil (Gotto) Neville-Rolfe – she is described as a feminist and a eugenicist and, alongside Francis Galton, she founded the Eugenics Education Society (which eventually became the Galton Institute in 1989). She also started the Imperial Society for Promoting Sex Education and organised the first International Eugenic Congress in London (1912). It is said that Neville-Rolfe was a feminist and committed to working in shelters for young women – her Christian morals compelled her to fight for an end to prostitution mainly as a fight against 'disease' and 'uncleanliness.' Her feminism compelled her to 'save' and 'rescue' 'those' women from themselves and the white Anglo-Saxon race from 'those women' and those like them. Imperial ideas of race shaped her thinking on eugenics and social reconstruction (as she called it) and she moved these ideas into pushing for feminist 'reform' and policy at the heart of Empire. *Educate destitute women about contraception. Eliminate prostitution. Some people are genetically superior. Women need financial independence. Some genetically advanced women need to marry and have children. Others don't need to have any children. If you don't have a decent house, job, marriage, health declaration, education, body, then you should not be allowed to have children.* [15] She was given an OBE. She did it all for the 'women'. You see what I mean?

14. For more see: Black feminist writing (such as Lorde, A. *Sister Outsider: Essays and Speeches.* 1984. Crossing Press; and hooks, b. *Ain't I a Woman : Black Women and Feminism.* 2015. Routledge); critiques of imperial and colonial feminism (such as Mohanty, C. *Under Western Eyes: Feminist Scholarship and Colonial Discourses.* 1988. Feminist Review, 30(1): 61-88; and Abu-Lughod, L. *Do Muslim Women Need Saving?* 2013. Harvard University Press); and detailed works on white feminism and race (such as Ware, V. *Beyond the Pale: White Women, Racism and History.* 1992. Verso; and Jonsson, T. *Innocent Subjects: Feminism and Whiteness.* 2021. Pluto Press)

15. I could not find a single detailed profile of Sybil Neville-Rolfe and instead got this information from bits and pieces on different websites

So I've given you some information on the complicity of politically active women (who might or might not have called themselves feminists) in Empire and eugenics at this time, but we can now go back to the suffragettes. The politically active women of the Edwardian period included both those for women's suffrage and those against suffrage. Many of the aristocratic and elite women saw the democratisation of socio-political life and the militancy of the suffrage campaigns as a threat to their class positions and what good is gender without class? But many women from the organisations listed above were also actively involved in the fight for suffrage. The imperial cause, Christian values and morals, and the unanimous understanding that 'women' were important united them all in spite of differing opinions on suffrage and on 'unwomanly' tactics to achieve it. There is your sisterhood. But is this really surprising? (or shocking as per the 'performance lecture'!) We know that the Women's Social and Political Union was an imperial organisation. We know that a large faction of this organisation (led by Emmeline Pankhurst) was in favour of stopping all campaigning for the women's vote to support the First World War. We know that universal suffrage was part of white feminist imperialism and the civilising mission. We know that many women in the Women's Social and Political Union and the fight for suffrage joined the British Union of Fascists.[16] We know that suffragettes like Rosa May Billinghurst (from the mural in Lewisham) stopped campaigning and all their political activity after the Representation of the People Act 1918. We know that only propertied women (over the age of thirty) got the right to vote from those campaigns and that act.

16. See more here – Pugh, M. *Why Former Suffragettes Flocked to British Fascism.* 2017. Slate.

Almost a decade ago, someone I lived with in a student hall during my PhD years organised a talk on feminist histories of the UK. The speaker was a white woman historian. I went to the talk. I was naïve. She did the two things that are often done in telling these histories. She erased the emergence, complicities and investments of these feminist and women's movements in white supremacy, colonial violence, and imperialism (as if gender and womanhood has ever been constituted without race). She didn't tell you a single thing about women's resistance in anti-colonial movements, about women who fought for freedom from Empire and from racism, about women in trade union movements and working class women fighting for the vote and much more, about Black women fighting white supremacy and patriarchy and imagining and realising queer kinships and worlds, about transnational sisterhoods between Black, brown, Muslim, colonised, migrant, working-class, disabled women who took care of each other across the oceans that were used to brutally supress their lives, about freedom and justice from colonialist capitalist patriarchy. What was left was exactly the kind of white gendered history that allows white women to stand proudly with placards that say ridiculous things like 'well behaved women rarely make history'. What women? What history? Not mine. Not ours.

Part III: Violence/Feminisms/Futures

I was teaching a module on (feminist, queer, crip, decolonial approaches to) violence when covid-19 was declared a global pandemic. Actually, I was on strike from teaching a module on (feminist, queer, crip, decolonial approaches to) violence when covid-19 was declared a global pandemic. As our industrial action to fight for working/learning conditions in higher education came to an end, the first lockdown seemed imminent in the UK, even though the government was advocating the eugenicist strategy of 'herd immunity' and the university itself was determined to stay 'business as usual'.[17] *Leave the pandemic unregulated and let the virus makes it way. Some vulnerable people can be shielded (who knows for how long and how exactly?) and the rest might and will get ill and die. No sick pay. No change in working and living conditions. The elderly, disabled, immunocompromised, hourly-paid, Black and PoC and working class communities - all disposable to the state. Only those with pre-existing conditions will be affected, we are told.* What was a pre-existing condition and vulnerability in a world structured by state violence and racial capitalism?

Our teaching moved online (while the institution was still attempting to force cleaning and security staff to come to campus) and we huddled on zoom to think through disablement, debility, and state violence in a pandemic. Black and PoC communities in the UK are worst affected, we are told; it is a genetic thing, the eugenicists declare; it is a socio-cultural thing, the white academics explain. Disabled people, yet again, are seen as expendable; their knowledges on illness, bodies, and mutual aid readily appropriated and extracted. They're being made to sign DNR orders and isolate with no/limited support.[18] What of those who are left out of the

17. Laterza, V. and Romer, L. P. *Coronavirus, herd immunity and the eugenics of the market.* 2020. Al Jazeera.

18. See - Sins Invalid. *Social Distancing and Crip Survival: A Disability Centered Response to COVID-19.* 2020. Sins Invalid Blog; and Blakeley, G. *The Government Abandoned Disabled People Long Before Covid.* 2021. Tribune.

category of sick/ill because of the racist, ableist, sexist, classist violence of the medical model of disability and what of those who are being/have always been forced to work while being sick/ill and what of those who are being made ill/sick because of work?

More than a year later, we still teach online; 150,000+ deaths in the UK and unending grief and loss; vaccine imperialism and global transnational state violence; uprisings against anti-Black police and state violence. We make connections. The pandemic has furthered the dangerous working conditions that sex workers have to face in the UK;[19] it has intensified the on-going violence towards trans and non-binary people – a combination of transphobic state measures and murderous austerity and horrific public discourse shaped by trans-exclusionary and so-called 'gender critical' feminists;[20] it has involved strengthening of border controls [apparently we only talk about opening borders when white middle class people *need* to go on holiday to Europe in the summer]. The PCSC Bill is read in parliament – giving more power to the police, regulating and even banning protests with a tighter grip, further criminalising GRT communities and those who have been made homeless.[21] The Nationality and Borders Bill is read in parliament – criminalising asylum seekers, putting them at higher risk of exploitation, trafficking, injury, and death.[22] We make connections – disposable lives, state violence, gender essentialism, eugenics, racial capitalism, a global pandemic. [What is a pre-existing condition again?]

We repeatedly visit the word 'feminism' – what does this even mean when Priti Patel is apparently a girl/boss is apparently a feminist is apparently even a 'woc' feminist is apparently a 'woc' 'daughter of migrants' feminist? When those with a politics of stifling and criminalising

19. Rosa, S. K. *Out of Work and Unsupported, Sex Workers Struggle to Cope With the Coronavirus Crisis.* 2020. Novara Media.

20. See more- Giles, H. J. *Trans in the UK: What the Hell Are We Going To Do?* 2021. Medium.

21. Lothian McLean, M. *#KillTheBill: Why we can't let the government ban protest.* 2021. gal-dem Magazine.

22. Rahman, M. *The gal-dem guide to Priti Patel's horrible new immigration bill.* 2021. gal-dem Magazine.

trans lives, constructing 'womanhood' as immutable [and white and middle class and able-bodied], and pushing for solidification of sex and gender essentialism are feminists? When those advocating for heightened policing and borders and for a world based on eugenicist logics do so in the name of feminism? We can talk about all this within the frameworks of feminisms and the far-right (unsurprisingly, the trans exclusionary feminists find allies frequently on the right[23]) or the frameworks of right-wing feminisms (remember, Thatcher, like Patel, was hailed as a feminist icon by many) or the historicising of these connections within conservatism (after all, as I talk about in the previous section, suffragettes have been known to speak about the strengthening of white supremacy with women's suffrage and supporting eugenicist and imperial/colonial projects, including the very project of white woman's suffrage).[24] However, if we are to resist this interconnected colonial capitalist violence and if we are to believe with every breath that "feminist work is justice work"[25] [and I hope we do] and if we are to build coalitions and solidarity, it is necessary to stop exceptionalising the right-wing and draw out the continuities and complicities of liberalism and fascism as they pertain to feminism, (White) Feminism (of all persuasions) as a political project developed within and through racial logics and continues to further them. A focus on right-wing women without centring these continuities and complicities is often a distraction [note to self: this applies transnationally] and the kind of distraction that allows white feminists to situate their histories within the left [and the kind of distraction that allows Indian upper caste feminists to situate their histories outside of caste-based violence].[26]

In 2017, Sisters Uncut reclaimed Holloway Prison's Visitor Centre in North London and transformed

23. For more see - Phipps, A. *Me, Not You: The Trouble with Mainstream Feminism*. 2020. Manchester University Press (especially Chapter 6: Feminists and the far right, pp. 133-159)

24. Ibid.

25. I am grateful to Lola Olufemi for this vision and grounding. See – Olufemi, L. *Feminism, Interrupted: Disrupting Power*. 2020. Pluto Press. (this quote is the title of the introductory chapter).

26. My past and current research examines women's mobilisations within the Hindu right-wing movement in India and Israeli Zionist settler project in Palestine and this piece is strongly shaped by that work.

this site of state violence into a week-long space of community, care, learning, and a collective abolitionist fight for survivors of domestic violence and against all forms of gendered and racialised state violence. Another world is very much possible.[27] In 2021, in a series of ongoing protests and actions, Sisters Uncut and various other activist groups stood together to Kill the (PCSC) Bill and to yet again show us that – a feminist fight is a fight against state and police violence in all forms, none of us are free until all of us are free, and that feminist work indeed is always justice work.[28] Another world is very much possible. As I try to bring this to an end, I am not even sure why I wrote this piece. [I ask the white artists (and myself) again – who is this even for?] The mess we are in today didn't appear out of nowhere. Your (white) sisterhood was never ours – it was premised on our oppression and erasure. Your glorious history of 'women's movements and feminist struggles' was and is an imperial history that continues to stifle and kill. The radical presents, futures, worlds, and freedoms that some of us dream of and make happen hold histories you will never be able to understand. The 'insistence of joy, of aliveness, of love and community' that we share is our revolutionary promise.[29] Another world is possible and always has been.

27. For more details, see - Press release: Feminists occupy Holloway Prison to demand more domestic violence services. 2017. Sisters Uncut; and Sisters Uncut Reclaim Holloway Prison: Addressing the legacy of state violence. 2017. Verso Books Blog.

28. For more, see the video of the Kill the Bill Public Meeting organised by Sisters Uncut. 18 March 2021. (https://www. facebook.com/sistersuncut/ videos/kill-the-bill-meeting/284475396454453/)

29. I borrow this quote from and remain immensely inspired by my student Ruari Paterson-Achenbach and their powerful and imaginative work submitted on the module I convened in Spring 2021. The piece was titled "A personal reflection on queerness, transphobia in the U.K. and thinking beyond" and emerged from and gave us/me ways to "move across, against, and beyond, towards glimpses and promises of otherwise and elsewhere".

Feminism: Notes on Dirt and Disgrace

Lola Olufemi

1.

The Act for the Abolition of the Slave Trade was signed by King George III in 1807. On the 15th April 1868, the Manchester National Society for Women's Suffrage held the first public meeting at Manchester Free Trade Hall. It is no wonder the vote could not account for all of us.

*

"We, the Housewives of Great Britain, are in open revolt against bread rationing. The rich people will not suffer, it's the middle classes, the poor people, the people with children, there's the ones that's going to suffer. It's bread for breakfast, bread for dinner, bread for tea for them. Therefore we, the British Housewives League, will not stand for bread rationing." Irene Lovelock, 1946.[1]

Lovelock takes the stage at a town-hall meeting. She is small, unassuming, bespectacled; received by a sea of respectable, middle class white women, with stern gazes and determined postures. The news reel calls them an 'army of indignant housewives.' The stuff of history. *harmless*, the prism of domesticity makes their complicity in facist mobilisation unthinkable.

*

The Empire begins to decline in 1945.

Whilst revolt is a daily necessity in the colonies and masses of women are resisting the exploitation inherent to the imperial mission, revolt is being wielded metaphorically by those who want the flag, nation, queen, country and good Christian values to remain firmly in place. What they call a revolt is really an attempt to capitalise on the growing momentum against women's subordination and wield it against the possibility of socialist governance. The words look strong, they rouse, they bite back. Make no mistake, these are demands made from the inside of the nuclear family by the property owning class. The race for enfranchisement before the black man is over. The British Housewives League: they call themselves guardians of the home. Key aims include showing "that over-control by the State is not in the interests of a free and happy home life and the development of personality in accord with Christian tradition."

*

In 1949, Claudia Jones will write *"To win the Negro women for full participation in the anti-fascist, anti-imperialist coalition, to bring her militancy and participation to even greater heights in the current and future struggles against Wall Street Imperialism, progressives must acquire political consciousness as regards her special oppressed status."*

Her words won't be excavated in the mid 1980s. She won't appear in the mainstream timeline of feminist history. There will be many debates about her 'erasure', liberals will call her the forbearer of intersectionality and the mother of Notting Hill Carnival, nobody will remember she was a communist.

*

Feminism is frequently a cause for embarrassment. What passes for feminist thought: the advancement of women and women's interests results in a history of entanglements with the right wing. Why did so many suffragettes become fascists? Well, the suffragette mission was a training ground for dictatorship. They were engaged in a war for the vote: they called their leader Emmeline Pankhurst, who noted dutifully in 1913, *"I'd rather be a rebel than a slave."* When the war ended, they moved on to the next mission. The past will say women were coerced and manipulated into Oswald's army, it will not say that their embrace of facism was a natural progression.

*

For some, this history feels sacrilegious. This is dirt, this is disgrace. This is airing history's dirty laundry. The British Union of Fascists offered a version of equality that did not relegate white women back into the realm of domesticity. It gave them tasks to do: regulate the nation with us, make tea for the men back in duty, canvas on the doorstep with bright eyes and even brighter smiles. Use your *womanly gifts* for good.

*

'Fascism... would treat the normal wife and mother as one of the main pillars of the State.' Moseley writes, women are useful insofar as they can be used as another part of the ideological apparatus. In the 1930s, up to 25% of the members of the British Union of Fascists were women.

*

The timeline strangles us. The thing about waves is, some of us end up washed up – some of us drown (sabotage commodity), others sail atop the sea in a straight line toward EQUAL RIGHTS. Drowning is not an act of feminist resistance, though.

When we begin with the suffragettes, we ellide the fact that the vote did not symbolise a desire to be free. They knew it could never give them that.

A certain history of feminism is obsessed with power. They realise that they look good in the uniform too, they can march, they can maintain order. We need to give women back the capacity for evil, some say. We need complex female characters they write over and over again. We need bad girls! *Well behaved women seldom make history.* But your history is full of bad girls. By that I mean, women who looked at Moseley's Blackshirts and thought, I want a slice of that pie. I want to have it all. *"I was first attracted to the Blackshirts because I saw in them the courage, the action, the loyalty, the gift of service, and the ability to serve which I had known in the suffragette movement,"* Mary Richardson explains.

They actively recruited women to the cause. This was no dripping tap, they went to lunches and tea rooms, to gala's and some place where they could talk quietly without the men. They said, woman – *will you restore Great Britain, do you care about the future of your country and your flag? Will you resist its desecration? What kind of subordination are you willing to endure? Join us, join us.*

Feminism. What a waste, those of us relegated to the realm of the unseen spend time fighting over the word.

The smart bypass the linguistic trap.

A feminist is [XXXXX] / she does [XXXXX] / most importantly, she believes in the equality of the sexes and sex as an immutable, biological fact and that women are *human beings*. We need more women statues please and NO gender neutral bathrooms and *courage calls to courage everywhere* and we need Austen on the banknote so little girls aspire to capital and gender is sex-role play but you can't say that nowadays and *A Woman's Place* is in the revolution (legal battles over the protection of hate speech) and *can't you see?!?!?* women are being colonised by gender ideology and queer theory.

Listen closely, can you hear the echoes?

*

Bad history is everyone's history. Yet, these tales of feminism seem strangely distant. Some lament their heroes fall from grace. But these aren't *my* people, this isn't my origin point, these references are alien to me. Feminism is a history of gatekeeping. Why do you think so many of us aim to escape the label, the name, the desire to be seen? Why do you think we want no part in what it was, what it has become?

*

The feminists I know are ready and willing to surrender power in the name of a liveable life. They'd give it all up if necessary. They are trying to get FREE, not even.

*

Many years later, the once revered white feminist thinker will be seduced by the so-called 'alt-right.' Her brothers in arms. Something something about how the woke mob burns women at the stake if they step out of line. Her comrades will try and call her back. She will decry and reject any allegiance to contemporary feminist thought. She will carefully slot herself back into the history that birthed her.

*

The sister to the fascist is no sister of mine. Global sisterhood died the second some of us were sacrificed to the linear progress narrative, the second we became fodder for debate.

*

In the gallery, two white women artists put whiteness on display. They invite feedback and reflection. They blow those fascists up so big, it's hard to not to think of them as monuments.

2.

THE SEX WARS were not really about power, or sex or even the male gaze. Maybe they were a battle over the totality of the imagination. Decades later, some of us can't escape fetish. Psh, some good the war did us.

THE SEX WARS should have been a fight over labour and working conditions: sex doesn't exist without them. The woman on the screen or full bushed in playboy magazine, the women on onlyfans or whose work is ripped from her website to feature (uncompensated) on the 'feminist' porn site are not an abstraction. They hate working just as much as you do.

*

When Dworkin writes *every woman's son is her potential betrayer,* she forgets the women she betrayed too.

*

How much of the sex wars was white panic about white bodies being consumed by white men. How much of the sex wars was protecting feminity as imbued in the body of white women, a desire to protect virtue, virginity's successor. Meanwhile, black women's bodies circulated for profit, sexual relief, to serve the boss and the master: the cornerstones of white supremacist violence. The history is there, you don't have to look hard to find it.

*

The leatherdykes can tell us about pain. Maybe sex and pain are portals to places outside of the body and normative sexuality and discourses on ontology.

The anti-pornography line was implicitely about regulation. Only certain acts are permissible, ban the perverse, drive out the undesirables. But undesirable means: lesbian perverts, femme tops, intersex angels, any number of f*gs, budding bottoms, bull dykes, lesbian mothers, drag queens, transexuals, cross-dressers, *anyone who likes a good time.*

*

In the 1980s they start rounding up gay men under Operation Spanner, they arrest some of them, charging them with assault occasioning actual bodily harm and unlawful wounding. Aids runs rampant. Did the anti-pornography feminists account for this? How their PANIC! might be refracted by the state and bounce back, shaping the public health approach that allowed a generation to perish.

*

Maybe THE SEX WARS were just a rehearsal for the next discursive battle that will take place. AI is getting more popular. We're safe now ladies!! the men are busy fucking robots and blow up dolls.

*

What do the border and THE SEX WARS have in common? Both require bodies to be reduced to their most essential parts - for transit, for discourse.

3.

WHEN I THINK OF WOMEN'S LIB, I THINK OF MEET-
ING SPACES WHERE POLITICAL CONSCIOUSNESS
GREW LEGS AND BURROWED INTO HEARTS AND
MINDS, I THINK OF "THANK YOU FOR SHARING
WITH US" AND "WE WILL KEEP YOU SAFE, YOU
DO NOT NEED TO GO BACK TO HIM, YOU DO NOT
DESERVE THIS" AND "WE MUST BEGIN TO NAME
AND ANALYSE OUR MATERIAL CONDITIONS IF WE
ARE TO BRING ABOUT THE NECESSARY ACTION
TO TRANSFORM THEM." I THINK OF WOMYN AND
AND ALL THE ATTEMPTS TO ESCAPE A LANGUAGE
WITH NO ESCAPE ROUTE AND LESBIAN SEPER-
ATISM, FOR ALL ITS ILLS. I THINK OF THOSE LES-
BIANS THAT ABSEILED INTO THE HOUSES OF PAR-
LIAMENT AND AUDRE LORDE'S READING GROUP
IN BERLIN, LEILA KHALED, THE PANTHER BREAK-
FAST SCHOOL PROGRAMME, I THINK OF OWAAD
AND BBWG AND SHEBA PRESS AND SABAAR
BOOKSHOP, I THINK OF THE ZAPATISTA'S, CYBER-
FEMINISTS, KURDISH FREEDOM FIGHTERS,
GRASSROOTS MOVEMENTS AGAINST DEPOR-
TATION, DETENTION AND SECTIONING, THE SEX
WORKER OCCUPATION OF SAINT-NIZIER CHURCH
IN LYON, I THINK OF THE EARLIEST GENDER FUCK-
ERS – THE WRITERS OF ANTI-CAPITALIST QUEER
AND TRANS MANIFESTOS, I THINK OF THE BLK ART
MOVEMENT AND TRANSNATIONAL CRIES FOR
SOLIDARITY FROM FEMINISTS ON THE WRONG
SIDE OF THE BORDER. I THINK OF BLACK SQUAT-
TERS AND OLIVE MORRIS AND 121 RAILTON ROAD.
I THINK OF HOW CRIP FEMINISM REVEALS THE WAY
EUGENICS UNDERPINS EVERYTHING, I THINK OF
THE COMMUNIST HORIZON AND FOWAAD! AND
HOW EVERYONE WAS A MARXIST.

THEN I REMEMBER FOR SOME PEOPLE THE HISTORY
OF WOMEN'S LIB IS ONLY SHEILA RAWBOTHAM
AND EQUAL PAY AND VIRAGO PRESS AND SEX
DISCRIMINATION ACTS... I SMILE FONDLY AT OUR
MISTAKES.

I THINK OF THE ONE BLACK LESBIAN WHO PLEADS
FOR A BLACK WOMEN'S CAUCUS, I THINK OF HOW
MANY MEMBERS OF THE LESBIAN LEFT NOW MIS-
TAKE WHO THE REAL ENEMY IS

I THINK OF THE BLACK FEMINISTS WHO WERE
MORE INTERESTED IN PAN-AFRICANIST REVO-
LUTION THAN GERMAINE GREER. I THINK OF HOW
BLACK FEMINISM IS ONLY EVER AN ABERRATION,
A DISRUPTION, A SECESSION, A CLEAVE IN THE
MANTRA OF FAKE UNITY. THEY WANT NOTHING
TO DO WITH THE TIMELINE. THEIR HISTORY IS
MAROONAGE AND ORGANISING AGAINST POLICE
VIOLENCE AND SUPPLEMENTARY SCHOOLS FOR
THEIR BETRAYED CHILDREN, THEIR HISTORY IS
INTERNATIONALISM AND CLASS AS INSEPARA-
BLE FROM RACE AND GENDER. THEIR HISTORY IS
REPRODUCTION IN A FREE WORLD, MAKING AND
UNMAKING EACH OTHER WITHOUT BIOLOGY, NOT
JUST ABORTION ON DEMAND.

WHEN I THINK OF WOMEN'S LIB, I REMEMBER
HOW SILLY IT IS THAT THE DESCENDENTS OF
SLAVE-OWNERS GATHERED TO DISCUSS BODY
HAIR AND CALLED THAT A REVOLUTION.

Top Girls and the Age of Tory Feminism

Juliet Jacques

On 13 July 2016, Theresa May was sworn in as Prime Minister of the United Kingdom by Queen Elizabeth II, becoming the second woman to take on the role. Back in 2005, as the MP for the safe seat of Maidenhead, May had co-founded Women2Win, a mentoring and pressure group within the Conservative Party to encourage the election of more Conservative women as MPs and their greater involvement in British public life. In her first Prime Minister's Questions, May moved to head off criticisms from Labour leader Jeremy Corbyn about the disproportionate impact of the Tories' austerity programme, imposed since their return to government in 2010, on women. Her response, obviously intended to become a slogan, was triumphant: "What does the Conservative Party do for women? It makes us Prime Minister!"[1]

1. Toynbee, P., Hazarika, A., Wallace, M. & Harker, J. *Theresa May's first prime minister's questions: our writers give their verdict.* 2016. The Guardian.

May was cheered on by columnists even from ostensibly left-wing or liberal newspapers, who had nothing to say about her previous position as Home Secretary, which she used to initiate a 'hostile environment' for immigrants to the UK, or her history of voting against an equal age of consent for non-heterosexual people, same-sex adoptions and the repeal of Section 28. The *Guardian's* Ayesha Hazarika called this 'a performance to make Tory MPs feel confident they picked the right leader', and *ConservativeHome* editor Mark Wallace gushed about how May 'embraced the inevitable comparison' to Margaret Thatcher, the first female Conservative leader and UK Prime Minister, 'on her own terms'.[2] With huge leads in opinion polls by the end of the year, May felt confident enough to call a snap General Election for June 2017. Hoping to give herself a large majority and enable her to put a Brexit deal through parliament, it did not turn out as she hoped: the slim majority won by David Cameron in 2015 became a hung parliament, after a campaign described as "inept" by a senior Tory MP in *Politico* magazine.[3]

2. Ibid.

3. McTague, T., Cooper, C. & Dickson, A. *How Theresa May Lost It.* 2017. Politico.

Pundits who had built up May as the new Thatcher instantly dropped her. In the same *Politico* article, Hazarika said the Tories' 'biggest mistake was to focus their campaign on May', and that 'anyone with "a modicum of objectivity" would have understood that May was not a "natural, confident, fluent performer *[and]* doesn't come alive in front of a crowd."'[4] But while May's campaign *had* been poor, characterised by reluctance (and often outright refusal) to talk to the press and a manifesto full of unpopular policies, her party still won its highest vote share since Thatcher was re-elected in 1983, with 42.4% (13.6 million people). The tight result was due to Corbyn cohering 40% of the electorate (12.8 million) around a Labour manifesto that promised to reverse the effects of austerity, turn back the Thatcherite privatisations and cuts to corporation tax that had been presented as political common sense for a generation or more, and allow younger people access to the arts and higher education.

The election basically killed May's premiership, which then had to be propped by a confidence-and-supply agreement with the anti-abortion, anti-equal marriage Democratic Unionist Party of Northern Ireland. It looked like May's brand of female-led, social and political conservatism was finished at the 2017 Conservative Party conference, in which she coughed her way through a speech to a small audience of (mostly) old and white people as letters from a party slogan fell off a wall behind her and a comedian handed her a P45. She clung onto the leadership until July 2019, after two years of failing, often spectacularly, to get a Brexit deal approved by the Commons, and was replaced by Boris Johnson – who had never apologised for earlier sexist remarks, referring to women as "hot totty", calling children of single mothers "ill-raised, ignorant and illegitimate" and

4. Ibid.

66

berating men for their inability to "take control of their women".[5] This looked like the end, at least for now, of May's Women2Win project – a failure that had looked unlikely, and certainly not inevitable in the early 1980s, as Thatcher cemented her ascent with the Falklands War victory in 1982 and a second electoral coronation the following year.

I want to explore the trajectory of C/conservative feminism through a reading of Caryl Churchill's play *Top Girls,* written in the wake of Thatcher's coming to power and first performed at the Royal Court Theatre in London in August 1982. A critical and commercial success that soon became a staple of Drama degrees and A-Level Theatre Studies courses (like the one I took in 1998-2000), the play centred around Marlene, a working-class woman who had repudiated her roots, proudly voted for Thatcher and fought her way to become the head of the female-led employment agency Top Girls (which might just as easily have been called 'Women2Win'). Men are discussed, but none are ever seen on stage: *Top Girls* is about how women relate to each other. It has three acts, taking place in a restaurant where Marlene dines with various notable women from literature, art and politics, as well as her office, and the home of her sister, Joyce.

Churchill wrote *Top Girls* at the end of a decade of female-empowerment when several Acts of Parliament had made abortion, contraceptives and divorce easier to obtain, equal pay for men and women in the same job had been secured and employers were obliged to guarantee pregnant women their job after maternity. The Seventies were also a time when male socialist playwrights such as Edward Bond, Trevor Griffiths and David Hare, as well as collectives such as Red Ladder, had made a huge

5. Woodcock, A. *Downing Street refuses to say if Boris Johnson regrets past sexist comments.* 2021. The Independent.

impact on British theatre, and feminist texts by Eva Figes, Germaine Greer and Kate Millett were paving the way for women – already becoming more prominent in journalism and broadcasting – to set up their own journals and publishing houses to support the Liberation Movement. The fact that very few women occupied high-paying jobs – just 2% of those in the top 2.5-3% of full-time 'high earners' in 1979, according to the Policy Studies Institute[6] – fed into a schism within this emergent feminist movement, between those who felt the capitalist system needed serious reform or revolution, and those who wanted to preserve it but make it more accessible to women – a categorisation which they tended not to break down further along class or racial lines.

6. Naismith, B. *Synopsis.* 1991. In: Churchill, C. *Top Girls.* Methuen: London, p.xxxii.

Before writing *Top Girls,* Churchill felt the more socialist approach to feminism in the UK was under threat. 'I had been to America, and had been talking to women there who were saying things were going very well: they were getting more women executives, women vice-presidents and so on': she wanted the first act of her play in particular to 'show that just to achieve the same things that men had achieved in capitalist society wouldn't be a good object'.[7] This ambitious first act put Marlene in a raucous dinner with Isabella Bird, a Victorian woman who had travelled the world; Emperor's courtesan and Buddhist nun Lady Nijo (b. 1258); Dull Gret, the subject of a painting by Brueghel who leads an army of women fighting devils in hell; Joan, who is thought to have become Pope disguised as a man in 854 and killed two years later when her secret was discovered; and Patient Griselda, the obedient wife from Chaucer's *Canterbury Tales.*

7. Ibid., p.xxii.

Exploring each character's experiences with sexist social structures and their decisions to resist or embrace them, this long opening scene puts different models of womanhood and femininity in dialogue with each other, showing older behavioural conventions that *had* to be challenged, but painting a pessimistic picture of the type of feminism best placed to supersede them. The dinner is a toast to Marlene becoming managing director of the agency, and she drinks to 'Our courage and the way we changed our lives and our extraordinary achievements'.[8] As the host, she is constantly talking, although there are certain subjects she refuses to address – she tells Isabella she has a sister but does not elaborate, and fends off questions about her love life. Certainly, her convivial and hedonistic demeanour contrasts notably with the only working woman: the waitress, who never speaks, and never receives a word of thanks for her service. The future of feminism, this suggests, has no class consciousness, and no place for solidarity – when concern is shown for the guests, it is because of the suffocating behaviour of the men in their lives. Patriarchy is the problem, stated most clearly by Isabella, who declares near the end that "I cannot and will not live the life of a lady"[9]. Throughout, it is implied that the world would be better if women like the guests ran it, but the issue of inequality is never raised. Without such awareness, the women are doomed to repeat the cruelty of their male oppressors.

The waitress aside, these women seem to see each other as friends, if not comrades, rather than competitors. This changes in *Top Girls'* more realist second act, which is set in the early 1980s and cuts between the agency – where we see the women in the office, and interviewing people for whom they hope to find work – and the home of Marlene's sister, Joyce. The interviews are a game of expectations management, starting with Marlene's conversation with Jeanine, who works as a secretary and doesn't know what she wants, beyond a new job.

8. Churchill, *Top Girls*, p13.

9. Ibid., p26.

After telling Jeanine not to tell potential employers she's married, and to change how she dresses, Marlene tries to push her into advertising, then a booming industry. (The Conservatives' decision to commission Saatchi & Saatchi to design their 1979 campaign materials – including the famous poster that said 'Labour isn't working' above an image of a long queue for an unemployment office – raised the Saatchis' profile, and increased the influence of the advertising industry in the UK.) Marlene does all she can to impress her mindset on Jeanine, imploring her to think about "where you want to be in ten years" and emphasising the need to be "confident".[10] Jeanine isn't sure she can summon this quality at will: Marlene tells her it's a matter of putting her mind to it, showing how the Thatcherite emphasis on individual responsibility reproduces itself in seemingly everyday scenarios.

10. Ibid., p32.

Throughout the second act, we see Churchill's warning from the first play out; copying patriarchal behaviours and striving to be part of the existing social order will not provide women with genuine equality, let alone a wider sense of fulfilment. Looking for a new position, Louise talks at length about being overtaken by younger women with 'a different style' who 'are not so careful' and 'take themselves for granted'.[11] As a result, she doesn't like working with women and feels she constantly has to prove herself, especially in her interview. Shona, meanwhile, desperately fills her CV with lies, first about her age (claiming to be 29, rather than 21) and then her career, delivering a long monologue about selling fridges that the interviewer instantly recognises as fraudulent. The implication here is that the new order promised by Thatcherism will be so ruthless that people – especially women, already disadvantaged because of the business world's entrenched sexism, that the agency are rightly trying to break down – are expected to lie, and lie *well,* to

11. Ibid., p52.

keep afloat, which will likely lead to long-term atrophy of every part of British public life, not to mention its economy.

The most striking scenes in Act Two, however, feature 16-year-old Angie, who has learning difficulties, and who lives with Joyce. First, we see Angie, bored, having a bleak, bad-tempered conversation with her friend, Kit, four years her junior. Angie bullies Kit and talks about killing 'my mother', Joyce, who works in four different cleaning jobs and struggles to bring up Angie on her own. This is the world that Marlene, having bought so totally into the business-driven feminist culture of the moment, has left behind, and about which she cannot bear to think. However, Marlene cannot avoid confrontation with it forever: Angie believes it is not Joyce who is her mother but Marlene, and goes to visit her office, seeing Marlene's world as more exciting than her own. Angie's lack of prospects is a constant concern for Joyce, and a source of stress and guilt for Marlene, who is visibly awkward in Angie's company and tells colleagues that her niece is 'a bit thick' and 'a bit funny' and that 'she's not going to make it'.[12] What Marlene means by this isn't clarified, but presumably that Angie is not going to have a career like Marlene's (and is thus, in Marlene's eyes, hopeless). Joyce has similar anxieties but frames them in terms of social issues rather than personal deficiency: she tells Angie's friend Kit that Angie is 'not going to get a job when jobs are hard to get' and worries Angie is 'one of those girls [who] might never leave home'.[13]

12. Ibid., p66.

13. Ibid., p43.

These anxieties about Angie's future bring out the conflict between the sisters: Marlene, who hated their working-class parents, blaming their father's personality (especially his drinking) for the family's circumstances, and Joyce, who says the problem was that their parents' 'lives were rubbish' and that Angie's will be too, 'because nothing's changed and it won't with *[the Conservatives]* in.'[14] Their contrasting feelings about the kind of society about to be fashioned boil over in the final scene, a conversation between the two in Joyce's kitchen just after the 1979 election, in which Marlene says 'the Eighties are going to be stupendous' and Joyce asks: for who?[15] Their bitter argument peaks with Marlene insisting that 'the working class doesn't exist any more ... it means lazy and stupid' and accusing Joyce of being jealous of her success, and the wealthy in general, before ranting about 'the reds'.[16] She tries to apologise after Joyce brings up Angie's prospects, but the bridge is broken – Marlene has chosen her career over her family, and the latter will not forgive her for focusing so ruthlessly on the former. This is a recurring theme throughout: the question of whether women can 'have it all' (i.e. both) is put to the audience, who are told Joyce had a miscarriage and Marlene two abortions. When Marlene did have a child, Angie (about whose father we are told nothing), she ultimately decided to leave her in Joyce's care: behind her apparent success is a huge lie, to her daughter and the wider world, and profound unhappiness.

Top Girls has aged well, largely because its prediction that the idea of social climbing – or 'social mobility' as the New Labour government tended to call it – would become hegemonic, crowding the language and politics of class out of mainstream discourse. Thatcher's politics is mirrored in Marlene's disdain for "the slimy unions", but even Marlene could not have imagined how comprehensive Thatcher's victory over the miners in 1984-85 would be, nor the promises by the next Labour Prime Minister to 'leave British law the most restrictive on trade unions in the Western world'.[17] Famously, Thatcher said New Labour was her greatest achievement:

14. Ibid., pp85-86.

15. Ibid., p83.

16. Ibid., pp85-86.

17. Gall, G.. *Blair's Trade Union Reform at 20.* 2020. Tribune.

her transformation of the British political landscape was so successful that the main opposition operated on her terms, and its supporting journalists bought entirely into the idea that representation of women within the system was more important than reforming it.

This was brought into stark focus in summer 2015, when Jeremy Corbyn stood, successfully, to become leader of the Labour Party on an anti-austerity platform. While Corbyn's long history of standing up for workers' rights and supporting the striking miners, and opposing apartheid, the Iraq war and Anglo-American foreign policy secured his support amongst those affected not just by widening inequality but the decimation of public services after the financial crisis of 2008 following the long-term deregulation of the banking industry that began under Thatcher, his politics threatened the political and media hegemony. Terrified pundits accused Corbyn and his supporters of everything under the sun, but one of the first lines of attack was that they were misogynists. When Corbyn announced the first-ever shadow cabinet containing more women than men, their line shifted, criticising the lack of women shadowing 'the four great offices of state' (of Prime Minister Home Secretary, Foreign Secretary and Chancellor).[18] Corbyn's defence was that this concept was out of date, from a time before women even had the vote, and that the positions he had given to women on health, education and employment rights played a more important role in empowering women.

18. Dathan, M. *Jeremy Corbyn comes out fighting amid sexism row and insists shadow Cabinet positions he has given to women are the real 'top jobs'.* 2015. The Independent.

This 'feminist' line of attack did not really stick, but given the decades-long hegemony of Thatcherism, it was not surprising that so many pundits lined up to support Theresa May over him, sounding at times like Marlene with her paranoid shrieking about flying pickets and being sent to Siberia. When Corbyn's Labour kept pushing the line that austerity had hit women the hardest – saying in March 2017 that welfare cuts since 2010 cost them £79bn in total, compared to £13bn for men – May responded by saying a Conservative woman had replaced a Labour man in a recent by-election.[19] What this meant for women at the sharpest end of society was left unclarified, May's 'feminist' credentials suffered and the election May called soon after effectively killed her premiership, and her Women2Win project, given her succession by Boris Johnson – a man described as "disrespectful" and "patronising" by women at the London Assembly during his time as the city's mayor, and who was reported to the police during the leadership race to succeed May in June 2019 when neighbours heard him shouting at his girlfriend, Carrie Symonds.[20]

May's main legacy has been to cement the idea that the Tories can use minorities to cover for policies that are disastrous for those minorities, especially those without wealth: currently holding May's former position as Home Secretary is Priti Patel, who notoriously admitted that her own parents might not have been allowed to move to the United Kingdom under the punitive, points-based immigration system introduced after the country finally left the European Union. This is an interesting contrast with David Cameron's promotion of openly gay Conservative MPs (with 12 in parliament in 2015), and his decision to push equal marriage into law in February 2013, backed by fewer than half of his MPs, with considerable opposition from the party membership. Cameron said he did this to make gay people, and gay culture, more conservative, allowing them to buy into heteronormative structures at a time when so much political rhetoric was targeted at 'hardworking families' – and covering for the fact that austerity had made waiting

19. Stewart, H. *Women bearing 86% of Commons austerity burden, Commons figures reveal.* 2017. The Guardian.

20. Gil, N. *A Brief History of Our New Prime Minister's Most Sexism and Homophobic Comments.* 2019. Refinery29.

lists for gender reassignment services far longer, and forced huge budget cuts for LGBT+ services nationwide.[21] This qualified, limited support for LGBT rights – one that broke with Thatcher and forced Theresa May to change her position on the issue – seems like another age now, after the Brexit referendum and the far-right ascendancy within the Conservative Party. Perhaps this, and the 'Women2Win' line of feminism will be redeployed if it suits the Tories to move back towards the centre-right politics of Cameron, but for now, May's project lies in ruins, and the best route for a woman to advance in her party would most likely to be by arguing *against* better representation for women, rather than for it.

21. Colgan, F., Hunter, C. & McKearney, A. *Staying Alive: The Impact of 'Austerity Cuts' on the LGBT Voluntary and Community Sector (VCS) in England and Wales.* 2014. TUC Funded Research Report.

Either way, *Top Girls* remains a perceptive dissection of how such representation works.. The hollowness of Marlene's career, and her growing pain as she is forced to confront the compromises on which she built it, stands for the hollowness of the right-wing feminist project as a whole, as the monetarism of the 1980s led to the financial crash of 2008 and the brutal austerity of the 2010s. As such, the play serves as a warning not to repeat this privileging of "making women Prime Minister" over improving the lives of working people, and not to allow the Conservatives to repeat the same trick with feminism, or with racial or sexual minorities. For all of Joyce's cynicism after Thatcher's ascent, it also serves as a powerful reminder not to give up on class politics in the wake of an electoral defeat: to do so will only empower the likes of Marlene further, and condemn people like Joyce and especially Angie to an increasingly bleak future.

I'm not a woman I'm a conservative

Acknowledgments

Special thanks to:
Jackson Bateman, Shaan Bevan, Mateo Villanueva
Brandt, Sacha Guedj Choen, Jack Clarke, Michael
Ditchburn, Rósza Farkas, Juliet Jacques, Kizza Kizza,
Peter Kosowicz, Dominic Sylvia Lauren, Thumbprint
Editions Ltd, Akanksha Mehta, Leonardslee
Gardens Doll's House Museum, Lola Olufemi, Vaso
Papadopoulou, Ruth Pilston, Owen Pratt, Aristea
Rellou, Sigg Art Residency, Justine Do Espirito Santo,
Pierre Sigg, 18 Stafford Terrace, Niina Ulfsak

Disgrace:
Feminism & the Political Right

Disgrace: Feminism and the Political Right
explores the history of conservative
feminism in the UK from the Edwardian
period to today. Expanding on Hannah
Quinlan and Rosie Hastings' research for
their eponymous exhibition, the book aims
to provide contextual information for the
viewer, both as a resource on the history
of feminism on the political right and to
provide a deeper historical and political
insight into the works within the exhibition.

Editors:
Ruth Pilston,
Hannah Quinlan & Rosie Hastings

Design:
Jack Clarke

Printing & Binding:
Gomer Press Ltd

Paper:
Colorplan 175gsm &
Arctic Matt 135gsm

Typography:
Monotype Grotesque Std &
URW Nimbus Roman

Edition:
500